S0-AZX-785

Text by Ron Thomson
Illustrations by Dave Klug

Published by Eastern National, copyright 2018.
ISBN 978-1-59091-198-3

Eastern National promotes the public's understanding and support of America's national parks and other public trust partners by providing quality educational experiences, products, and services. Visit us at www.eParks.com.

Printed on recycled paper.

OUR NATIONAL PARKS

The first national park in the world, Yellowstone National Park, is now more than 145 years old.

Today, there are more than 400 parks in the U.S. National Park System. Some trace our national history. Others honor famous people. There are parks that preserve natural features and wildlife. Every park offers activities for mind and body. Together, they reflect the places and ideas we value as a nation.

We should be proud of our National Park System. Countries around the world have copied the idea. The way we handle our national treasures sets a standard for others to study. The people who work in national parks keep the system strong. Every day they study, protect, and teach about the parks in their care. They are not able to take care of our parks alone. You play a big role too. National parks exist for you. You can enjoy them, but you also must help protect them. When you visit, step lightly on the land. Think about our history. Take the Junior Ranger pledge to explore, learn, and protect. You can help make sure every one of these special places is around forever.

UNITED STATES GEOGRAPHICAL PASSPORT REGIONS

WASHINGTON
MONTANA
NORTH DAKOTA
MINN.
MAINE
OREGON
IDAHO
SOUTH DAKOTA
WISCONSIN
VT.
N.H.
MASS.
N.Y.
CONN.
R.I.
WYOMING
MICHIGAN
IOWA
PA.
N.J.
NEVADA
UTAH
COLORADO
NEBRASKA
OHIO
MD.
DEL.
D.C.
W. VA.
CALIFORNIA
KANSAS
MISSOURI
ILLINOIS
IND.
KY.
VA.
ARIZONA
NEW MEXICO
OKLAHOMA
ARK.
TENN.
N.C.
S.C.
MISS.
ALA.
GEORGIA
TEXAS
LA.
FLA.
ALASKA

GUAM   HAWAII

U.S. VIRGIN ISLANDS

PUERTO RICO

- North Atlantic Region
- Mid-Atlantic Region
- National Capital Region
- Southeast Region
- Midwest Region
- Southwest Region
- Rocky Mountain Region
- Western Region
- Pacific Northwest and Alaska Region

How To Use Your Passport

Your Junior Ranger Passport will show you the many different types of national parks there are. You'll discover that parks preserve and protect our history, natural areas, and wildlife.

There are also parks where you can do fun things, and others where you can learn about the people who helped shape our country. Some parks are well known like the Grand Canyon and Statue of Liberty. There are many more that are not as well known. Sleeping Bear Dunes sounds like a place worth a visit. How about Craters of the Moon or Wind Cave? Once you start looking, you may never stop visiting.

Olympic NP

Like the regular Passport To Your National Parks book, the Junior Ranger Edition is divided into geographic sections. It highlights many of the parks found in each region and shows what makes each region special. A map shows where all the parks are located, and there is a list that you can check once you have visited a park.

Park Cancellations

Bring your book with you when you visit a park to get it canceled. In each of the regional sections, there are pages to collect park cancellations. This ink mark will show the name of the park and the date you visited.

Cape Hatteras National Seashore
AUG 14 2018
Nags Head, NC

JUNIOR RANGER CANCELLATIONS

There are also pages where you can collect Junior Ranger cancellations. You get one of these by completing the Junior Ranger program at the park you are visiting.

Complete the program at the park, and a park ranger will stamp your Junior Ranger Passport book!

JUNIOR RANGER PASSPORT STICKERS

Another fun activity you can do is to collect the special Junior Ranger Passport stickers. There is a set that comes with the book. There are nine stickers on the set, one for each Passport region.

Peel off the sticker and place it on the regional sticker page.

ANNUAL SET OF JUNIOR RANGER PASSPORT STICKERS

There is also a set of Junior Ranger Passport stickers that is issued once a year. This set will feature parks from each region that are having an anniversary or celebrating a special event. They are available at participating national parks or by visiting **www.eParks.com**.

See page 102 for park abbreviations key.

"EXPLORE, LEARN, AND PROTECT"

The National Park Service helps protect special places for everyone to enjoy now and in the future. You can also help take care of these important places.

Join the National Park Service "family" as a Junior Ranger. Promise to protect parks, learn about parks, and share park stories with friends and family.

HOW DO I BECOME A JUNIOR RANGER?

1. Visit a national park with your family, friends, scout troop, or other group.
2. Get a Junior Ranger booklet at the park's visitor center.
3. Complete the activities.
4. Let a ranger check your booklet.
5. Take the Junior Ranger pledge.
6. Receive an official Junior Ranger badge and certificate.

While most Junior Rangers are ages 5 to 13, people of all ages can take part.

WHY BECOME A JUNIOR RANGER?

Some become Junior Rangers because they want to help protect nature and animals. Maybe you learned about national parks at school. Maybe you're looking for a fun way to explore new places and ideas. After you get one badge, you'll want to get more, visit more parks, and learn why each one is special.

WHAT KINDS OF ACTIVITIES WILL I DO?

It's always a surprise. You might hike to odd rock formations. There could be games to help you learn about desert plants and animals. Maybe you'll see fossils. What kinds of animals live along the beach or in caves? How much does the Liberty Bell weigh? How were the lives of historical figures like yours? How were they different? Becoming a Junior Ranger is only step number one. Keep exploring, learning, and protecting. Pass on what you've learned.

JUNIOR RANGERS EXPLORE WITH ALL THEIR SENSES

One of the best things about national parks is that they invite you to use all five of your senses.

You'll **see** amazing cave formations and incredible rock shapes. What does a natural river **sound** like? Enjoy the surprisingly sweet **smell** of ponderosa pines. Have you ever **tasted** pure water right from a spring? What does a hawk feather **feel** like?

JUNIOR RANGERS CONTINUE TO LEARN

Junior Rangers never stop learning. They stay curious. If that happens, you'll learn about flight and fossils, volcanoes and Valley Forge. You can learn about whatever interests you by exploring national parks.

PROTECT OUR SPECIAL PLACES

Junior Rangers understand it's important to care for and protect special places, plants, and animals. We all need them for a balanced and healthy future.

WHAT IF I CAN'T VISIT A NATIONAL PARK?

Don't worry. The WebRangers program gives you a chance to earn badges, patches, and special rewards online. New activities are added all the time. It's a great way to learn about parks that are far away.

VISIT WWW.NPS.GOV/WEBRANGERS

STEWARDSHIP

Park rangers and other people who work for the National Park Service are stewards of our parks. A steward protects and cares for something they feel is important and worth preserving. When you become a Junior Ranger, you too become a steward of the parks. What are some ways Junior Rangers can be good stewards for the national parks?

WHAT IT MEANS TO BE A JUNIOR RANGER

Being a Junior Ranger is more than just completing fun activities and collecting badges. It's an exciting way to learn about different historic figures, places, nature and wildlife, and sharing the things you learn with your family and friends. When you explore nature and history in our national parks you'll discover new, meaningful connections with these very special places. That's why it's important to protect the treasures found in our national parks!

LEAVE NO TRACE

When you're out exploring parks, make sure to practice "Leave No Trace" principles.

- Dispose of waste properly, keep the park clean.
- Know and follow park regulations.
- Stay on trails to keep from damaging plants and vegetation.
- Leave what you find, don't take any natural or cultural artifacts from the park.
- Respect wildlife, observe from a distance and don't feed them.
- Be considerate of others, keep noise levels down when hiking or camping.

You can also find information online about Junior Ranger programs. Go to **www.nps.gov** and search for the park you want to visit. The park's homepage should have a link that says "Learn About the Park," and underneath it a tab for "Kids & Youth." Here you'll find lots of information about Junior Ranger programs and other activities.

As the parent of a Junior Ranger, I promise to:

Encourage exploration of the wonders around us, engage my Junior Ranger in active learning each day, and support opportunities for kids and families to get outside and have fun.

Together, Junior Rangers and their families will enjoy and preserve America's natural and cultural resources for generations to come.

The following pages show how our national parks preserve America's natural beauty, history, and wildlife. Our parks tell the stories of the people who helped shape our country and are great places to have fun!

NATURAL BEAUTY

Our national parks preserve some of the most beautiful places on Earth.

Olympic NP

National parks have the tallest mountains in the United States. The peak of Denali is over 20,000 feet high. In contrast, Badwater Basin sits on the dry, parched floor of Death Valley NP almost 300 feet below sea level. Rain seldom falls on wind-swept deserts at Bandelier NM, Joshua Tree NP, or Arches NP. But waves never stop washing the beaches of national seashores and lakeshores. There still are wild, churning rivers that reshape their valleys.

Acadia NP

The redwood trees at Redwood NP, Yosemite NP, Muir Woods NM, and Sequoia & Kings Canyon NP are not just big but very old. Cacti at Joshua Tree NP and Saguaro NP grow taller than most people. The prairie grasses at Tallgrass Prairie N PRES look fragile waving in the wind, but have a tough tangle of roots 8 to 14 feet deep in the ground. Did you know that wetlands like those at Assateague Island NS have a greater number of plants and animals than most places on Earth? And don't forget that you can see all sorts of plants close to home. Parks in or near big cities grow wild plants too.

Rocks and minerals are the main attraction at many parks. At Hawai'i Volcanoes NP, the lava from volcanoes creates new land before your eyes. The mountains at Denali NP and Mount Rainier NP are some of the tallest on Earth. When you climb to the top of Cadillac Mountain in Acadia NP, you can greet the sun rising over the Atlantic Ocean. On the Pacific Coast, Olympic NP begins at the edge of the ocean and reaches glaciers on Mount Olympus almost 8,000 feet up. Wind and water reshape colorful rocks and dig deep canyons like those at Canyonlands NP, Bryce Canyon NP, Zion NP, and of course, Grand Canyon NP. In the spring, when the water runs high, the jagged,

Redwood NP

rocky bottom of New River Gorge NR makes frothy waves and churning rapids. Fire Island NS, Cape Hatteras NS, Cumberland Island NS, and Padre Island NS contain sandy islands that protect homes along the coast. The cliffs at Pictured Rocks NL have streaks of black, white, red, yellow, brown, pink, and green. There are more than 4,700 caves in national parks. At least four are more than 130 miles long. You can explore caves at Mammoth Cave NP, Wind Cave NP, Carlsbad Caverns NP or Jewel Cave NM.

Glacier NP

DRAW YOUR OWN SCENE OF NATURAL BEAUTY!

Capitol Reef NP

Muir Woods NM

Virgin Islands NP

I HAVE SEEN:

- ○ Mountains
- ○ Lakes
- ○ Rivers
- ○ Forests
- ○ Deserts
- ○ Oceans
- ○ Prairies
- ○ Valleys
- ○ Caves
- ○ Sunsets
- ○ Full Moons
- ○ _____
- ○ _____
- ○ _____
- ○ _____

America's national parks are the oldest, tallest, largest, longest, hottest, smallest, wildest, rainiest, coldest, lowest, and most spectacular places in the United States!

- Denali NP has the tallest peak in the United States at 20,310 feet.

- Mammoth Cave NP is the longest known cave system in the world. There are more than 400 miles of caves in the park!

- Gateway Arch at Gateway Arch National Park is the tallest monument in the United States at 630 feet!

- Crater Lake NP is the deepest lake in the United States at 1,943 feet.

- Death Valley NP is the hottest place ever recorded in the world at 134 degrees in 1913. It's also the lowest at 282 feet below sea level.

- Great Smoky Mountains NP is one of America's most biodiverse areas. In 800 square miles, more than 19,000 species have been documented.

HISTORY

There are national parks from the pages of every chapter of U.S. history.

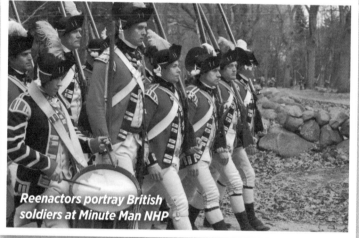

Montezuma Castle NM

Reenactors portray British soldiers at Minute Man NHP

Many parks focus on American Indians, Alaska Natives, and Native Hawaiians. Charcoal found at Russell Cave NM is from 10,000-year-old campfires. Objects linked to the Hopewell Culture were well-made and highly prized. Artisans at Pipestone NM still carve dark red stones to make pipes. In the West, the Sinagua people built the large cliff homes at Montezuma Castle NM. There are 26 known pictograph sites in Santa Monica Mountains NRA. You can see replica totems at Sitka NHP. The arrival of settlers from Europe changed the lives of American Indians no matter where they lived.

Spanish explorers like Hernando de Soto roamed the South and Southwest for over 200 years. The long journey of Lewis and Clark in 1804-1806 opened the nation's eyes. So much land! Settlers moved inland from the East through mountain passes at Cumberland Gap. Wagon trains traveled trails to the West. Native people defended their way of life, which lead to conflicts at places like Little Bighorn Battlefield NM and Big Hole NB. Millions from around the world came to America.

Many saw the Statue of Liberty before they passed through Ellis Island and later settled in every state in the nation.

As the 13 colonies grew, so did ideas about how to make laws and protect people's rights. Colonial NHP, Independence NHP, and Federal Hall N MEM show how the United States was born. How did it break apart? There are dozens of Civil War sites from Fort Sumter NM to Appomattox Court House NHP to help you understand. What happened after the war? Reconstruction Era NM looks at how the North and South reunited. Women's Rights NHP, César E. Chávez NM, and Stonewall NM trace the struggle for equality.

At Golden Spike NHS, you'll learn how Chinese immigrants helped build the railroads. At Salem Maritime NHS and New Bedford Whaling NHP, you can learn about sailors

Women's Rights NHP

Thomas Edison

and sea captains who sailed around the globe. They brought shiploads of trade goods into ports. Great inventors like the Wright brothers mastered flight, while Thomas Edison developed the phonograph and movie camera.

Young people made history too. Girls worked in cotton mills in Lowell, Massachusetts. Boys and girls walked to class at Little Rock Central High School guarded by soldiers.

TIMELINE OF IMPORTANT EVENTS IN YOUR LIFE

DATE

EVENT

In CONGRESS, July 4, 1776.

A DECLARATION

BY THE REPRESENTATIVES OF THE

UNITED STATES OF AMERICA,

IN GENERAL CONGRESS ASSEMBLED.

[facsimile of the Declaration of Independence text]

Signed by ORDER and in BEHALF of the CONGRESS,

JOHN HANCOCK, PRESIDENT.

The Declaration of Independence declared our freedom from England....

IF YOU COULD DECLARE NEW RULES FOR OUR COUNTRY, WHAT WOULD THEY BE?

1:

2:

3:

4:

5:

6:

7:

NATIONAL PARK RANGERS

Protecting our national parks is an important job!

There are more than 20,000 proud employees of the National Park Service. That includes park rangers, maintenance workers, law enforcement rangers, historians, administrative staff, and biologists. They help keep these amazing places safe and beautiful. You are most likely to see interpretive park rangers when you visit. What do they do?

Park rangers are full of information and have amazing stories to share. They can tell the story of a mountain, a forest, a river, or a desert. They can tell the story of a bison, a bear, an eagle, or an alligator. They tell the stories of big battlefields and historic houses. They tell stories of remarkable individuals, cultures, and groups of people. Every national park story is important and deserves to be heard. What's your favorite national park story?

Most park rangers have been all over the country and have worked in many different types of parks. You can find park rangers in visitor centers, roving the trails, leading tours, and giving talks at campgrounds. They know all about a park's history and love to share their knowledge with Junior Rangers! The next time you see a ranger, ask him or her where they have been and what their favorite park is.

ACTIVITIES AND RECREATION

National parks are great for getting away, exploring, and for seeing and experiencing new things.

Our national parks seem to inspire visitors to be better in different ways. Parks are good for people, are scenic, historic, and pollution free. Plus, there are so many opportunities and things you can do.

How about challenging your body? Most parks have walking trails. Some are easy, while others are rugged. If you hike to the top of the volcano at Capulin Volcano NM at the right time of year, you can see migrating ladybugs. Go deep into the earth at Grand Canyon NP or high

Point Reyes NS

up onto a glacier at Mount Rainier NP. You can snowshoe your way through Valles Caldera N PRES on a trail, or you can travel all the way from Georgia to Maine on the Appalachian NST.

You don't have to go far to visit national parks. City parks are great places to walk. Hot Springs NP has 26 miles of trails. Plan to follow the Freedom Trail at Boston NHP.

If you and your family like to camp, you have many parks to choose from. There is Acadia NP and Delaware Water Gap NRA in the Northeast, Great Smoky Mountains NP and Dry Tortugas NP in the South, Voyageurs NP along the Great Lakes, Badlands NP and Channel Islands NP in the West, and Denali NP in Alaska.

For fun on the water, you can swim or canoe at many parks. Maybe you like rivers, bays, and lakes? Try Kenai Fjords NP, Isle Royale NP, Grand Teton NP, Ozark NSR, or Lake Mead NRA. If you'd rather go to a seashore or lakeshore, try Cape Cod NS or Point Reyes NS. Want to do a little fishing? Try Delaware Water Gap NRA, Chickasaw NRA, or Obed WSR.

For birdwatchers, a national park is one of the best places to be. Plan a trip to Big Cypress N PRES, Apostle Islands NL, Olympic NP, Point Reyes NS, or the treasure trove of wildlife found at Everglades NP.

The dark skies above Death Valley NP, Big Bend NP, Zion NP, and Glacier NP are great places to marvel at all the stars. National parks put on terrific light shows at sunrise and sunset.

National parks also provide outlets for creativity. At Weir Farm NHS, try your hand at art. At Edgar Allan Poe NHS, think about the stories you might tell. Do you have musical ability? Visit New Orleans Jazz NHP. Are you a budding cook? See what tasty dishes you can make at Jean Lafitte NHP. To have fun and stretch your brain, complete a Junior Ranger program, take the pledge, and get your badge and cancellation!

ACTIVITIES I HAVE DONE:

- _____
- _____
- _____
- _____
- _____
- _____
- _____
- _____
- _____
- _____

NATIONAL PARK SERVICE

Color in the Arrowhead.

The Arrowhead

The Arrowhead emblem you see on a park ranger's uniform is the official logo of the National Park Service. Each object depicted on the Arrowhead represents something that rangers are sworn to protect! The bison and the sequoia are plants and wildlife, the mountains and water represent beautiful scenery and recreation, and the Arrowhead outline represents historical and archaeological values.

IF YOU COULD DRAW A NEW LOGO FOR AMERICA'S NATIONAL PARKS, WHAT WOULD IT LOOK LIKE?

CREATE YOUR OWN SLOGAN:

I _____
national parks!

Go _____
a mountain!

Nature is for
_____!

I'm a history
_____!

I'd rather be
_____!

PETS IN PARKS

Did you know there are pet-friendly parks? In these parks, our furry friends can enjoy many outdoor activities with us.

Every park has different rules about where pets are allowed. Some parks allow pets almost everywhere. Other parks only allow pets in certain areas. Roads, trails, parking lots, campgrounds, and picnic areas are some areas pets may be allowed. **Check the pet rules before you go.**

PROTECT NATURE AND WILDLIFE

Some pets like to run and chase other animals. Dogs that chase or bark can make wildlife feel scared or threatened. Delicate plants can be crushed by an excited dog. Keep pets close to you on a leash no longer than six feet.

PROTECT OUR PETS

Our pets are curious. They like to explore every turn and sniff every bend. They don't stop to think how sharp rocks, spiky plants, or hot sand might hurt their feet. Keep pets safe by staying on approved trails. Choose only pet-friendly campgrounds. Don't forget to bring water and treats. Now you're ready to hit the trail!

WILDLIFE

The wildlife at national parks comes in all shapes and sizes.

Bobcat

There are animals with fur and feathers. Some are huge and others are tiny. They live everywhere from beach dunes to tall mountains, and from the desert to cloud-covered forests. Creatures live in oceans, creeks, and earthy burrows.

Some parks are famous for their animals. Yellowstone NP, Katmai NP, Glacier NP, and Yosemite NP have grizzly bears. Acadia NP has black bears. There are herds of grazing bison and frolicking pronghorn antelope at Wind Cave NP. Caribou roam Kobuk Valley NP. You can see majestic elk in Rocky Mountain NP. Bighorn sheep scramble over the rocky slopes of Colorado NM. At Yosemite NP, mountain lions stalk prey at night. During the day, mule deer graze on valley grasses.

It's easy to mistake a coyote for a wolf. The coyote is smaller and thinner. Wolves disappeared from many parks. They had to be resettled in Yellowstone NP. Coyotes on the other hand have learned to live almost everywhere.

Not all furry animals are large. Badlands NP has prairie dogs and black-footed ferrets. Many parks have beaver and fox. In the evening, bats pour out of

Elk at Point Reyes NS

Carlsbad Caverns NP looking for insects. Assateague Island NS is known for its wild horses.

National parks are great places to bird watch. There are bald eagles, peregrine falcons, and Northern goshawks in Lassen Volcanic NP. Every coastal park is alive with birds. Some live there year round, but many migrate to different locations.

Black bears

There are 425 species of birds in Big Bend NP. Don't forget the pink flamingoes of Everglades NP.

To see the largest and smallest creatures in national parks, dive into the world of water animals. Watch whales from Cabrillo NM. See sea turtles at Canaveral NS. Olympic NP has jellyfish, sea stars, and sea sponges. Many parks have rainbow or brown trout. If you've never seen a manatee, visit Big Cypress N PRES. The coral reefs in Biscayne NP and Virgin Islands NP contain colorful algae.

Keep in mind that national parks provide safe haven for many vanishing animals. Everglades NP protects the Atlantic hawksbill turtle and American alligator. The rare Louisiana pine snake, Louisiana black bear, and red-cockaded woodpecker live in Big Thicket N PRES. Several birds are endangered. Apostle Islands NL protects the piping plover and Point Reyes NS is home to the northern spotted owl. It would be sad to lose any of these creatures.

WILDLIFE I HAVE SEEN:

- ○ _____
- ○ _____
- ○ _____
- ○ _____
- ○ _____
- ○ _____
- ○ _____

- ○ _____
- ○ _____
- ○ _____
- ○ _____
- ○ _____
- ○ _____
- ○ _____

Cardinal

FIELD NOTES

Rangers use field notes to write down observations. Write down some of your observations from your park visits below.

Deer

STAYING SAFE IN PARKS

As a visitor to a national park, you're responsible for your own safety. Do your homework before you visit and learn the park rules.

Follow the information, advice, and warnings of park rangers and park staff. Then go have some fun!

WILDLIFE SAFETY

Respect wildlife. We're visitors in their home. View wildlife from a safe distance. What's a safe distance? At least 100 yards (about the length of a football field) away from bears and wolves. Stay 25 yards away from bison, elk, and other animals. Increase this distance if you see an animal change behavior.

If you're going to bear country, take bear spray.

Never try to pet or pick up a wild animal. Don't feed wildlife, even if they beg.

If you treat wildlife with respect by not approaching or feeding them, you are helping them live natural lives.

CAMPING SAFETY

Animals are attracted to food smells. Lock all food and cooking items in your car or a storage locker. Put trash in animal-resistant dumpsters. Don't take food inside your tent.

HIKING SAFETY

Know your limits and do what's right for you. Don't push yourself or your group members to hike, climb, or explore beyond their physical abilities. Plan what to do if someone becomes separated from your group. Bring drinking water. Stay on the path. Obey warning and safety signs. Use good judgment.

AMERICAN HEROES

National parks tell the stories of people from all walks of life.

Clara Barton was a nurse during the Civil War and founded the American Red Cross. Edgar Allan Poe, Carl Sandburg, and Henry Wadsworth Longfellow were authors and poets. Eugene O'Neill wrote plays. John Muir was an author who loved and was inspired by nature. J. Alden Weir painted soft, colorful landscapes. Sculptor Augustus Saint-Gaudens recreated eagles in flight, and heroic soldiers marching into battle. Frederick Law Olmsted designed parks with rolling, grassy fields.

Ben Franklin was a printer. Later he studied science and made all sorts of useful inventions. One hundred years later, Thomas Edison followed in Franklin's footsteps as an inventor. The Wright brothers made bicycles and then airplanes. Charles Young became a colonel. Eleanor Roosevelt earned the title "First Lady of the World" for her work on human rights. Martin Luther King, Jr., and Roger Williams fought for freedoms.

The men and women honored at national parks

Carl Sandburg Home NHS

Mount Rushmore N MEM

are as different as the colors of a rainbow. Alexander Hamilton was an immigrant who helped shape the U.S. Constitution. Jean Lafitte helped save New Orleans from the British army during the War of 1812. They started life enslaved, but Booker T. Washington went on to start a college and Frederick Douglass gave advice to Abraham Lincoln. Juan Rodríguez Cabrillo explored the West Coast for Spain. Maggie L. Walker ran a bank. César E. Chávez led a movement that changed farming.

The longest list of people honored by national parks are U.S. presidents. George Washington, Thomas Jefferson, Franklin D. Roosevelt, and Abraham Lincoln have sites that honor them across the country. Well-known presidents Harry S Truman, Dwight D. Eisenhower, John F. Kennedy, and Jimmy Carter all have parks named after them as do lesser-known presidents Martin Van Buren, James A. Garfield, and William Howard Taft. Perhaps the most famous presidential site is Mount Rushmore N MEM with four huge stone carvings of Washington, Jefferson, Lincoln, and Theodore Roosevelt.

Ben Franklin

Women's Rights NHP commemorates the struggle for equal rights led by Elizabeth Cady Stanton and Lucretia Mott. Harriet Tubman was a former slave who fought for abolition and equal rights for all.

Harriet Tubman

WHO WOULD YOU PUT ON MOUNT RUSHMORE?

Paste a photo or draw in who you think belongs on Mount Rushmore.

VOTE FOR
_____

ELECT
_____
FOR
_____

Fill in the blanks on these campaign buttons.

WHICH AMERICAN HEROES WOULD YOU LIKE TO MEET?

1: _____

2: _____

3: _____

4: _____

5: _____

6: _____

7: _____

8: _____

9: _____

10: _____

HOW YOU CAN BE AN AMERICAN HERO

Junior Rangers pledge to protect the special places included in the National Park System. What does that really mean? Does the pledge end when a Junior Ranger leaves a park?

As good stewards, Junior Rangers become people of action. When they give their word to protect our national treasures, they become guardians of the future. Their pledge follows them home.

That's important. It's great to get a Junior Ranger badge at a park. To really deserve it, a Junior Ranger needs to live it. They should respect land, air, water, plants, animals, and history all across the country. Every day, everywhere.

HERE ARE SOME THINGS THAT EVERY JUNIOR RANGER CAN DO:

1) Recycle, not just when visiting a park but at home and school.
2) Respect and care for not only the biggest or the cutest animals but for even the smallest of nature's creatures. The lives of each are linked to the health of all.
3) Help to keep water and air clean. Learn about pollution and how to stop it.
4) Learn about the mix of human experiences that makes our history so interesting. Respect others. Listen.
5) Get involved in a local project. Help improve the environment. Join. Contribute your talents. Become a part of the solution!

The following pages highlight the parks in each of the nine Passport To Your National Parks regions.

NORTH ATLANTIC REGION

The parks in the North Atlantic region tell us a lot about American history.

Saratoga NHP

John F. Kennedy NHS

Upper Delaware SRR

MAINE

VERMONT

NEW HAMPSHIRE

MASSACHUSETTS

NEW YORK

CONNECTICUT

RHODE ISLAND

CONNECTICUT
1. Weir Farm NHS

MAINE
2. Acadia NP
3. Appalachian NST
4. Katahdin Woods and Waters NM
5. Saint Croix Island IHS

MASSACHUSETTS
6. Adams NHP
7. Boston African American NHS
8. Boston Harbor Islands NRA
9. Boston NHP
10. Cape Cod NS
11. Frederick Law Olmsted NHS
12. John Fitzgerald Kennedy NHS
13. Longfellow House – Washington's Headquarters NHS
14. Lowell NHP
15. Minute Man NHP
16. New Bedford Whaling NHP
17. Salem Maritime NHS
18. Saugus Iron Works NHS
19. Springfield Armory NHS

NEW HAMPSHIRE
20. Saint-Gaudens NHS

NEW YORK
21. African Burial Ground NM
22. Castle Clinton NM
23. Eleanor Roosevelt NHS
24. Federal Hall N MEM
25. Fire Island NS
26. Fort Stanwix NM
27. Gateway NRA
28. General Grant N MEM
29. Governors Island NM
30. Hamilton Grange N MEM
31. Harriet Tubman NHP
32. Home of Franklin D. Roosevelt NHS
33. Martin Van Buren NHS
34. Sagamore Hill NHS
35. Saint Paul's Church NHS
36. Saratoga NHP
37. Statue of Liberty NM
38. Stonewall NM
39. Theodore Roosevelt Birthplace NHS
40. Theodore Roosevelt Inaugural NHS
41. Upper Delaware SRR
42. Vanderbilt Mansion NHS
43. Women's Rights NHP

RHODE ISLAND
44. Blackstone River Valley NHP
45. Roger Williams N MEM

VERMONT
46. Marsh-Billings-Rockefeller NHP

Saugus Iron Works NHS

Check the list above if you have...
- Visited Park
- Completed Junior Ranger Program

31

For thousands of years, many tribes of American Indians called this area home. They lived on what nature offered. Parts of Acadia NP, Katahdin Woods and Waters NM, and Cape Cod NS still look the way they did 400 years ago.

Then quickly, their lives changed. Ships with newcomers from France and England dropped anchor along the coast. Log villages appeared and grew into towns, and towns became small cities like Boston. The newcomers took over Indian land.

In the 1770s, the English settlers told the King of England they wanted to make their own laws. When the King said no, war broke out. Minute Man NHP and Adams NHP tell stories that show how war changed life for families.

The armies at the Battle of Saratoga were not only British and American, but also German. Finally, America won the Revolutionary War! George Washington was sworn in as first president of the United States at Federal Hall; and a new country was born.

While most citizens of the new United States farmed, others made things. At Saugus Iron Works, they made tools and horseshoes. In a few years, mills powered by water crowded riverbanks. At Lowell, you needed

Boston NHP

Whaling ship

Lowell mill girls

earplugs to keep the noise of the looms from hurting your ears. Young girls worked next to these machines day after day. About 100 miles away, Springfield Armory designed and made guns for the U.S. Army. *IN THE MIDDLE OF THE 1800s, SHIPS SAILED FROM NEW BEDFORD, THE WHALING CAPITAL OF THE WORLD. EVERYONE WANTED WHALE OIL FOR THEIR LAMPS, AND THE BRIGHT, WHITE FLAMES THAT WHALE OIL CREATED CHASED AWAY THE NIGHT.*

More and more people came from all over the world to live in the United States. As a young man, Alexander Hamilton moved to New York from the island of Nevis. He fought in the war against England, and became a national leader. African Burial Ground NM tells the stories of African men, women, and children brought to New York City, mostly as slaves, between 1690 and 1790. From 1855 to 1890, over eight million people entered the U.S. through the old fort at Castle Clinton NM. From 1892 to 1954, another 12 million passed through Ellis Island. Check

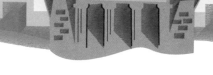

The Statue of Liberty

Revolutionary War soldiers

designed famous parks for everyone to enjoy. Henry Wadsworth Longfellow wrote poems about the past that schoolchildren would stand in front of class and recite. Maybe you know the poem about the ride of Paul Revere?

You will be amazed at the way the Vanderbilt family lived. Their 54-room mansion is filled with things that cost a fortune. Marsh-Billings-Rockefeller NHP preserves the home of Mary and Laurance Rockefeller. Their estate is a model of how to care for the forest and land. Other parks, like Stonewall NM and Women's Rights NHP, focus on how we treat one another.

to see if your relatives were among them. After 1875, everyone who sailed into New York harbor passed the Statue of Liberty and her lifted torch, showing them the way to freedom.

Artists and authors also made history. Saint-Gaudens NHS preserves the home and studio of sculptor Augustus Saint-Gaudens. Artists Thomas Cole and J. Alden Weir loved to paint in the country. Their art is filled with the same sunlight and autumn colors you will see on a fall day. Architect Frederick Law Olmsted

FIRST LADY ELEANOR ROOSEVELT WORKED ALL HER LIFE FOR EQUAL RIGHTS FOR ALL.

Eleanor Roosevelt

NORTH ATLANTIC REGION STICKERS AND PHOTOS

Place your North Atlantic Region Stickers (or any other stickers) on this page. You may also use this page to collect photos of your park trips or of the park rangers you meet!

Put Your North Atlantic Region Official Park Cancellations Here!

PUT YOUR NORTH ATLANTIC REGION OFFICIAL JUNIOR RANGER CANCELLATIONS HERE!

MID-ATLANTIC REGION

In the Mid-Atlantic states, geography is linked to history.

PENNSYLVANIA

NEW JERSEY

DELAWARE

MARYLAND

WEST VIRGINIA

VIRGINIA

Delaware Water Gap NRA

Morristown NHP

Gettysburg NMP

Regional Parks I Have Visited

Delaware

① First State NHP

Maryland

② Antietam NB
③ Assateague Island NS
④ Catoctin Mountain Park
⑤ Chesapeake and Ohio Canal NHP
⑥ Clara Barton NHS
⑦ Fort McHenry NM & HS
⑧ Greenbelt Park
⑨ Hampton NHS
⑩ Harriet Tubman Underground Railroad NHP
⑪ Monocacy NB
⑫ Piscataway Park
⑬ Potomac Heritage NST
⑭ Thomas Stone NHS

New Jersey

⑮ Gateway NRA
⑯ Great Egg Harbor SRR
⑰ Morristown NHP
⑱ Paterson Great Falls NHP
⑲ Thomas Edison NHP

Pennsylvania

⑳ Allegheny Portage Railroad NHS
㉑ Delaware Water Gap NRA
㉒ Edgar Allan Poe NHS

Assateague Island NS

㉓ Eisenhower NHS
㉔ Flight 93 N MEM
㉕ Fort Necessity NB
㉖ Friendship Hill NHS
㉗ Gettysburg NMP
㉘ Hopewell Furnace NHS
㉙ Independence NHP
㉚ Johnstown Flood N MEM
㉛ Steamtown NHS
㉜ Thaddeus Kosciuszko N MEM
㉝ Upper Delaware SRR
㉞ Valley Forge NHP

Virginia

㉟ Appomattox Court House NHP
㊱ Arlington House, The Robert E. Lee MEM
㊲ Assateague Island NS
㊳ Booker T. Washington NM
㊴ Cedar Creek and Belle Grove NHP
㊵ Colonial NHP
㊶ Fort Monroe NM
㊷ Fredericksburg & Spotsylvania NMP
㊸ George Washington Birthplace NM
㊹ George Washington Memorial Parkway
㊺ Great Falls Park
㊻ Jamestown NHS
㊼ Maggie L. Walker NHS
㊽ Manassas NBP
㊾ Petersburg NB
㊿ Prince William Forest Park
(51) Richmond NBP
(52) Shenandoah NP
(53) Wolf Trap National Park for the Performing Arts

West Virginia

(54) Bluestone NSR
(55) Gauley River NRA
(56) Harpers Ferry NHP
(57) New River Gorge NR

Check the list above if you have...

Visited Park

Completed Junior Ranger Program

Historians portray Revolutionary War soldiers at Valley Forge NHP.

The region's rivers are old but strong. It took eons for the Delaware River to cut through mountains to create the Delaware Water Gap. The deep river brought settlers and trade. A map of Philadelphia, the biggest American city in the 1770s, shows buildings all along the riverbank. *BECAUSE THE CITY SAT IN THE MIDDLE OF THE 13 COLONIES, CONGRESS DECIDED TO MEET THERE, IN INDEPENDENCE HALL.* This is where they wrote the Declaration of Independence in 1776. This started the Revolutionary War. Nearby, you can see the site of Ben Franklin's home. Franklin invented many useful items and discovered electricity.

During the winter of 1777-78, George Washington's army camped at Valley Forge. In the spring, his newly trained soldiers marched into battle. The area between Philadelphia and New York earned the nickname Crossroads of the American Revolution. Washington kept his army at Morristown, New Jersey, for the winter of 1779-80. After the war, in the 1830s, Philadelphia became a crossroads for writers, too. Author Edgar Allan Poe moved into a small brick house on the edge of the city where he wrote some of his best stories.

Where there are rivers, there are often mountains, trails, and valleys.

Independence Hall

Steam locomotive

They fought where the valley led, at Antietam and Gettysburg. There were only 100 miles between the capitals of the North and South. Places such as Manassas, Fredericksburg, Petersburg, and Richmond became deadly battlefields. Peace only returned when Confederate General Robert E. Lee surrendered to Union General Ulysses S. Grant at Appomattox Court House in 1865. *IN THE SHENANDOAH VALLEY, THE FAMILY OF A BOY NAMED BOOKER T. WASHINGTON HEARD THEY WERE FINALLY FREE.*

Rather than hike over mountaintops, people followed flat valleys. In the early 1800s, as people moved west, mountains blocked their path. A few places like Cumberland Gap became gateways between east and west. At Allegheny Portage, steam-powered machines pulled canal boats over a mountain on railroad cars. Even the big locomotives, like those at Steamtown NHS, could not climb mountains. Early industries clustered near rivers. Nineteenth-century factories preserved at Harpers Ferry NHP and Paterson Great Falls NHP used water for power and travel.

From Shenandoah NP you can see a wide valley that Civil War soldiers used when marching to battle.

The George Washington Memorial Parkway preserves scenery along the Potomac River. Jamestown was one of the first colonies in the new world. The British army surrendered to

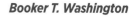
Booker T. Washington

General George Washington at Yorktown in 1781, ending the War for Independence. During the War of 1812, Francis Scott Key watched from a ship anchored in the bay as the British attacked Fort McHenry. The words he wrote about what he saw became our national anthem.

Ulysses S. Grant and Robert E. Lee meet at Appomattox Court House

tools, metal stoves, pots, and pans.

There is one more special place worth a visit. Flight 93 N MEM contains a field planted with wildflowers. It's a place that might make you sad, but proud. It's a place of honor. It marks the spot where Flight 93 crashed on September 11, 2001.

Assateague Island NS sits along the coast. You can see the famous wild horses there. The island looks thin and fragile, but it protects the mainland from waves whipped up by storms.

In the 1700s, England, France, and many American Indian tribes fought over who would own the land. In the early 1800s, places like Hopewell Furnace glowed with burning charcoal. Melted iron cooled to become

Flight 93 N MEM

MID-ATLANTIC REGION STICKERS AND PHOTOS

Place your Mid-Atlantic Region Stickers (or any other stickers) on this page. You may also use this page to collect photos of your park trips or of the park rangers you meet!

PUT YOUR MID-ATLANTIC REGION OFFICIAL PARK CANCELLATIONS HERE!

NATIONAL CAPITAL REGION

The capital
of our nation—
Washington, D.C.—
is a city of memories.

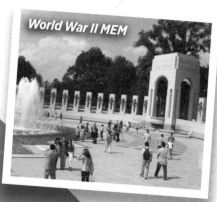
World War II MEM

Thomas Jefferson MEM

Rock Creek Park

DISTRICT OF COLUMBIA

VIRGINIA

MARYLAND

14 10 18 21 3 7 9 16 2 13 12 1 19 4 17 6 11 8 15 5 20

DISTRICT OF COLUMBIA

1. Belmont-Paul Women's Equality NM
2. Constitution Gardens
3. Ford's Theatre NHS
4. Franklin Delano Roosevelt MEM
5. Frederick Douglass NHS
6. Korean War Veterans MEM
7. Lincoln MEM
8. Lyndon Baines Johnson Memorial Grove on the Potomac
9. Martin Luther King, Jr. MEM
10. Mary McLeod Bethune Council House NHS
11. National Capital Parks - East
12. National Mall & Memorial Parks
13. Old Post Office Tower
14. Rock Creek Park
15. Thomas Jefferson MEM
16. Vietnam Veterans MEM
17. Washington Monument
18. White House
19. World War II MEM

MARYLAND

20. Fort Washington Park

VIRGINIA

21. Theodore Roosevelt Island

Check the list above if you have...
- Visited Park
- Completed Junior Ranger Program

Fireworks over the National Mall

Regional Parks I Have Visited

REGIONAL PARKS I HAVE VISITED

It's filled with statues and monuments. There are old buildings and museums. All over the city there are clues as to what we value most. It's a good place to think about the past and wonder about the future.

Martin Luther King, Jr. Memorial

You can't miss the white marble memorials that honor George Washington, Thomas Jefferson, and Abraham Lincoln. John Wilkes Booth shot President Lincoln in 1865 during a play at Ford's Theatre. At the Franklin Delano Roosevelt Memorial, you can read the president's famous words. At a time when many people could not find jobs and were fearful of what the future would hold, the president said, "the only thing we have to fear is fear itself."

Don't miss the stories of African American leaders. THE WHITE GRANITE STATUE OF MARTIN LUTHER KING, JR. STANDS 30 FEET HIGH. That's 10 yards on a football field. Dr. King's arms are crossed. His eyes stare ahead. He looks strong and steady. A quote reads, "Out of the Mountain of Despair, a Stone of Hope." Learn about the father of Black History Month, Carter G. Woodson, and see where he helped make history at Carter G. Woodson Home NHS. In the 1800s, Frederick Douglass was one of the great civil rights leaders. Visit his home at Frederick Douglass NHS. For several decades in the early 20th century, Mary

Alice Paul

McLeod Bethune fought for the rights of African American women.

Other sites in the capital remind us that everyday men and women make history. As a country, we honor them too. Belmont-Paul Women's Equality NM tells the story of Alice Paul and the National Woman's Party and the demand for equal rights for women. We honor the men and women who fought around the world during World War II, Korea in the 1950s, and Vietnam in the 1960s. From the edge of the city you can walk for 184 miles along the Chesapeake and Ohio Canal. For almost 100 years, starting in 1831, the canal was a major route for trade and travel.

The hushed silence at the city's memorials is very different from the hustle and bustle of the crowds that come to the National Mall for protests or celebrations. Along Pennsylvania Avenue you may see a parade or a presidential motorcade. Maybe you will join a march for something you believe in. The city, and

Korean War Veterans MEM

the parks it contains, plays a vital role in the life of our nation.

Before you leave, you should enjoy Washington's natural world too. There are miles of trails on Theodore Roosevelt Island. The 1,700 acres of Rock Creek Park and the path along the river in Anacostia Park are peaceful retreats. To relax, President Lyndon Johnson went to a spot on the Potomac River that is now a memorial grove named for him. You can learn about rivers and keeping water clean at Kenilworth Park & Aquatic Gardens. These natural places make memories too. They point to a better tomorrow for all.

Washington Monument

Franklin Delano Roosevelt MEM

National Capital Region Stickers and Photos

Place your National Capital Region Stickers (or any other stickers) on this page. You may also use this page to collect photos of your park trips or of the park rangers you meet!

PUT YOUR NATIONAL CAPITAL REGION OFFICIAL PARK CANCELLATIONS HERE!

PUT YOUR NATIONAL CAPITAL REGION OFFICIAL JUNIOR RANGER CANCELLATIONS HERE!

SOUTHEAST REGION

Parks in the Southeast have many big stories to tell.

KENTUCKY

29
31

30

55

58

54

56

TENNESSEE

61

59
57

60

38 43

NORTH CAROLINA

42 45

39

40

44

41

49 51

52 SOUTH CAROLINA

48

47
50

5

21

4

32

35 36

MISSISSIPPI

1 2
3

6 7

26 20
27

GEORGIA

28

53

24

66

65

VIRGIN ISLANDS

64 63 62

37

ALABAMA

19
25

23
22

18

15

11

16

10

46

PUERTO RICO

34

33

17

FLORIDA

12

8 9

14

13

Cumberland Gap NHP

Gulf Islands NS

ALABAMA
1. Birmingham Civil Rights NM
2. Freedom Riders NM
3. Horseshoe Bend NMP
4. Little River Canyon N PRES
5. Russell Cave NM
6. Tuskegee Airmen NHS
7. Tuskegee Institute NHS

FLORIDA
8. Big Cypress N PRES
9. Biscayne NP
10. Canaveral NS
11. Castillo de San Marcos NM
12. De Soto N MEM
13. Dry Tortugas NP
14. Everglades NP
15. Fort Caroline N MEM
16. Fort Matanzas NM
17. Gulf Islands NS
18. Timucuan E & H PRES

GEORGIA
19. Andersonville NHS
20. Chattahoochee River NRA
21. Chickamauga and Chattanooga NMP
22. Cumberland Island NS
23. Fort Frederica NM
24. Fort Pulaski NM
25. Jimmy Carter NHS

26. Kennesaw Mountain NBP
27. Martin Luther King, Jr. NHP
28. Ocmulgee NM

KENTUCKY
29. Abraham Lincoln Birthplace NHP
30. Cumberland Gap NHP
31. Mammoth Cave NP

MISSISSIPPI
32. Brices Cross Roads NBS
33. Gulf Islands NS
34. Natchez NHP
35. Natchez Trace Parkway
36. Tupelo NB
37. Vicksburg NMP

NORTH CAROLINA
38. Blue Ridge Parkway
39. Cape Hatteras NS
40. Cape Lookout NS
41. Carl Sandburg Home NHS
42. Fort Raleigh NHS
43. Guilford Courthouse NMP
44. Moores Creek NB
45. Wright Brothers N MEM

PUERTO RICO
46. San Juan NHS

SOUTH CAROLINA
47. Charles Pinckney NHS
48. Congaree NP
49. Cowpens NB
50. Fort Sumter NM
51. Kings Mountain NMP
52. Ninety Six NHS
53. Reconstruction Era NM

TENNESSEE
54. Andrew Johnson NHS
55. Big South Fork NRRA
56. Fort Donelson NB
57. Great Smoky Mountains NP
58. Manhattan Project NHP
59. Obed WSR
60. Shiloh NMP
61. Stones River NB

VIRGIN ISLANDS
62. Buck Island Reef NM
63. Christiansted NHS
64. Salt River Bay NHP & EP
65. Virgin Islands Coral Reef NM
66. Virgin Islands NP

Check the list above if you have...
Visited Park
Completed Junior Ranger Program

By visiting parks in this region, you can see how people from different places lived side by side. At Russell Cave NM, Ocmulgee NM, and the Natchez Trace Parkway, you can learn about the native people who lived here thousands of years ago.

After Columbus arrived in this new land, others followed. The flags of England, France, and Spain flew over frontier forts and villages like those at San Juan, De Soto, Fort Caroline, Fort Raleigh, Castillo de San Marcos, and Fort Frederica.

Russell Cave NM

The Africans brought to the United States as slaves came with customs, beliefs, and ways of life that are still honored today. During the Civil War, Roanoke Island became a refuge for freed slaves. Many joined the Union army. Parks like Reconstruction Era NM, Birmingham Civil Rights NM, Freedom Riders NM, Selma to Montgomery NHT, and Martin Luther King, Jr. NHP, follow the story of freedom from the 1860s to the 1960s.

When the colonies went to war against England, they won an early victory at Moores Creek in 1776. Hard fighting at Kings Mountain, Cowpens, Ninety Six, and Guilford Courthouse helped win the Revolutionary War. During the War of 1812, over 800 Creek Indian warriors died fighting

San Juan NHS

General Andrew Jackson and his troops at Horseshoe Bend.

War broke out again in 1861 at Fort Sumter when the Southern states chose to fight over their right to enslave African workers. This and other differences started the Civil War. Many families lost their crops, farm animals, and homes. Battles at Stones River, Shiloh, Chickamauga, Chattanooga, and Vicksburg showed how bloody war could be. New, more powerful

Civil War soldiers

weapons forced Fort Pulaski to surrender. Andersonville NHS honors the 13,000 men who died at the Civil War prisoner of war camp here.

DURING WORLD WAR II, AFRICAN AMERICAN PILOTS LEARNED TO FLY FIGHTER PLANES AT AN AIRPORT IN TUSKEGEE NOT FAR FROM THE COLLEGE STARTED BY BOOKER T. WASHINGTON, TUSKEGEE INSTITUTE. You can visit Manhattan Project NHP to learn about the science that created bombs used for massive destruction.

Throughout the region, you can see the many faces of nature. For mountains, visit Great Smoky Mountains NP

Tuskegee Airmen

Blue Ridge Parkway

and the Blue Ridge Parkway. Push a boat into the water and go with the flow of the Chattahoochee River. Deep underground, visit the world's longest cave at Mammoth Cave NP. Congaree NP, Big Cypress N PRES, and Everglades NP provide wetland homes for rare plants and animals. Without these parks, they might all vanish.

Maybe you like sandy beaches. Each wave changes the shape of barrier islands at Cape Lookout

NS, Cumberland Island NS, Canaveral NS, and Gulf Islands NS. You can dive to see coral reefs at Biscayne NP. The Timucuan Indians made their homes in the dunes, salt marshes, and nearby forests on Florida's coast. The black and white design on a lighthouse tells sailors they are near Cape Hatteras NS. In 1903, the Wright brothers used brisk winds off the ocean to lift the airplane they made by hand into the air.

Off the coast, at Buck Island Reef NM, Virgin Islands NP, and Virgin Islands Coral Reef NM, you can swim to coral reefs in the clearest, bluest water you have ever seen!

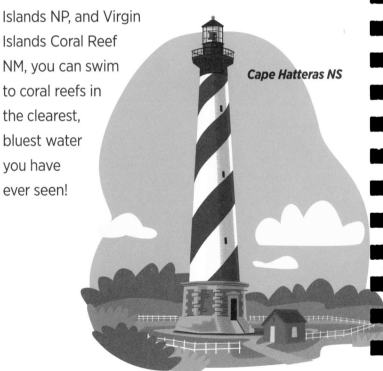

Cape Hatteras NS

SOUTHEAST REGION STICKERS AND PHOTOS

Place your Southeast Region Stickers (or any other stickers) on this page. You may also use this page to collect photos of your park trips or of the park rangers you meet!

PUT YOUR SOUTHEAST REGION OFFICIAL PARK CANCELLATIONS HERE!

PUT YOUR SOUTHEAST REGION OFFICIAL JUNIOR RANGER CANCELLATIONS HERE!

MIDWEST REGION

The Midwest features Great Lakes and homes of U.S presidents.

Lincoln Boyhood N MEM

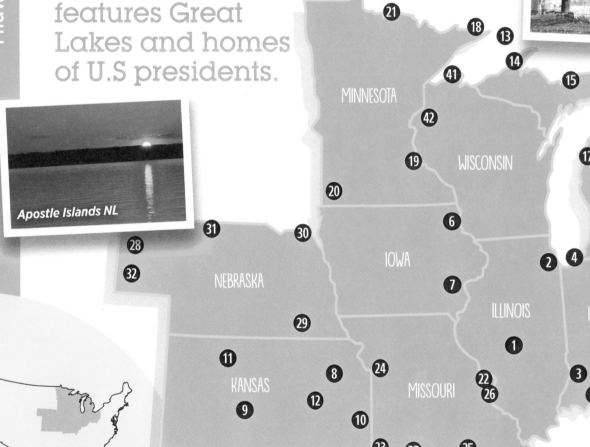

Apostle Islands NL

MINNESOTA

WISCONSIN

MICHIGAN

IOWA

NEBRASKA

ILLINOIS

INDIANA

OHIO

KANSAS

MISSOURI

Harry S Truman NHS

ILLINOIS
- ➊ Lincoln Home NHS
- ➋ Pullman NM

INDIANA
- ➌ George Rogers Clark NHP
- ➍ Indiana Dunes NL
- ➎ Lincoln Boyhood N MEM

IOWA
- ➏ Effigy Mounds NM
- ➐ Herbert Hoover NHS

KANSAS
- ➑ Brown v. Board of Education NHS
- ➒ Fort Larned NHS
- ➓ Fort Scott NHS
- ⓫ Nicodemus NHS
- ⓬ Tallgrass Prairie N PRES

MICHIGAN
- ⓭ Isle Royale NP
- ⓮ Keweenaw NHP
- ⓯ Pictured Rocks NL
- ⓰ River Raisin NBP
- ⓱ Sleeping Bear Dunes NL

MINNESOTA
- ⓲ Grand Portage NM
- ⓳ Mississippi NRRA
- ⓴ Pipestone NM
- ㉑ Voyageurs NP

MISSOURI
- ㉒ Gateway Arch NP
- ㉓ George Washington Carver NM
- ㉔ Harry S Truman NHS
- ㉕ Ozark NSR

- ㉖ Ulysses S. Grant NHS
- ㉗ Wilson's Creek NB

NEBRASKA
- ㉘ Agate Fossil Beds NM
- ㉙ Homestead NM of America
- ㉚ Missouri NRR
- ㉛ Niobrara NSR
- ㉜ Scotts Bluff NM

OHIO
- ㉝ Charles Young Buffalo Soldiers NM
- ㉞ Cuyahoga Valley NP
- ㉟ Dayton Aviation Heritage NHP
- ㊱ First Ladies NHS
- ㊲ James A. Garfield NHS
- ㊳ Hopewell Culture NHP
- ㊴ Perry's Victory and International Peace MEM
- ㊵ William Howard Taft NHS

WISCONSIN
- ㊶ Apostle Islands NL
- ㊷ Saint Croix NSR

Grand Portage NM

Check the list above if you have...
- ⬤ *Visited Park*
- ⬜ *Completed Junior Ranger Program*

Many parks in the Midwest are nestled around the Great Lakes. Both the Saint Croix and Cuyahoga rivers flow toward the lakes. Saint Croix NSR is wild and untamed. Cuyahoga Valley NP is a refuge for nature and preserves a historic route for trade and settlement.

The edges of the lakes, where land and water meet, can be fun to explore. **NATURE STREAKED THE COLORFUL CLIFFS OF PICTURED ROCKS NL WITH BLACK, RED, BROWN, AND YELLOW.** Sleeping Bear Dunes NL got its name from an American Indian story about a mother bear and her cubs. There are 21 islands to discover on Apostle Islands NL. Indiana Dunes NL has 15 miles of sandy beach and

windswept dunes. Even today, Isle Royale NP is rugged and remote. Wolves and moose both live on the island. As one hunts the other, both animals play an important role in the cycle of life on the island.

The name for Voyageurs NP comes from the French trappers who paddled far into the Ojibwe homeland. On their return, they packed bundles of beaver pelts into their 36-foot-long bark canoes. Until the early 1800s, these trappers met at Grand Portage to trade their goods. During the War of 1812, American sailors won the Battle of Lake Erie. The British no longer ruled the Great Lakes. Perry's Victory and International Peace Memorial celebrates peace instead of war.

Pictured Rocks NL

Effigy Mounds NM

many tribes. Control of frontier land played a big role in the War of 1812. Warriors led by Tecumseh won a victory in 1813 at River Raisin. Fort Larned and Fort Scott were outposts in the Indian Wars in the 1800s. Colonel Charles Young commanded the Ninth and Tenth U.S. cavalry. They were African American troops called "Buffalo Soldiers." Young later became the first African American superintendent of a national park.

In the history of the Midwest, many chapters are tied to people on the move. Visit Hopewell Culture NHP and Effigy Mounds NM to learn about American Indian trade routes. Tribes living near the Gulf of Mexico owned copper and stone objects they brought from the Midwest. Pipestone NM preserves the place where American Indians have crafted spiritual objects for centuries.

As settlers moved onto Indian lands, they caused unrest. Fighting broke out with the French, British, and

Fur trappers

65

Gateway Arch NP

Gateway Arch NP honors all who moved west. *BEGINNING IN 1862, HOMESTEAD ACTS GAVE AWAY MILLIONS OF ACRES.* Homestead NM of America tells us of the hardships the settlers faced. George Washington Carver grew up at a time when people fought over whether new states would allow slavery.

More and more, travelers switched from wagons to railroads. Pullman NM is the site where the Pullman company made railroad cars. Dayton Aviation Heritage NHP explains how the Wright Brothers perfected the airplane.

American history ties U.S. presidents to the Midwest. Two sites, Lincoln Boyhood N MEM and Lincoln Home NHS, shed light on the life of Abraham Lincoln. Ulysses S. Grant lived at the family home of his wife from 1854 to 1859. James A. Garfield campaigned for president in 1880 from the front porch of his Ohio home. If you go to Cincinnati, Ohio, you can see the home of William Howard Taft. Born in a two-room cottage, Herbert Hoover lost both his parents before he turned 10. Harry S Truman moved into the house of his childhood sweetheart Bess Wallace. He never thought of anywhere else as home.

Homesteader's hut

MIDWEST REGION STICKERS AND PHOTOS

Place your Midwest Region Stickers (or any other stickers) on this page. You may also use this page to collect photos of your park trips or of the park rangers you meet!

PUT YOUR MIDWEST REGION
OFFICIAL PARK CANCELLATIONS HERE!

MEM
2018
Midwest Region

PUT YOUR MIDWEST REGION
OFFICIAL JUNIOR RANGER CANCELLATIONS HERE!

SOUTHWEST REGION

You can learn a lot about building things by visiting parks in the southwestern United States.

El Malpais NM

Buffalo NR

Hot Springs NP

ARKANSAS

1. Arkansas Post N MEM
2. Buffalo NR
3. Fort Smith NHS
4. Hot Springs NP
5. Little Rock Central High School NHS
6. Pea Ridge NMP
7. President William Jefferson Clinton Birthplace Home NHS

LOUISIANA

8. Cane River Creole NHP
9. Jean Lafitte NHP & PRES
10. New Orleans Jazz NHP

NEW MEXICO

11. Aztec Ruins NM
12. Bandelier NM
13. Capulin Volcano NM
14. Carlsbad Caverns NP
15. Chaco Culture NHP
16. El Malpais NM
17. El Morro NM
18. Fort Union NM
19. Gila Cliff Dwellings NM
20. Manhattan Project NHP
21. Pecos NHP
22. Petroglyph NM
23. Salinas Pueblo Missions NM
24. Valles Caldera N PRES
25. White Sands NM

OKLAHOMA

26. Chickasaw NRA
27. Washita Battlefield NHS

TEXAS

28. Alibates Flint Quarries NM
29. Amistad NRA
30. Big Bend NP
31. Big Thicket N PRES
32. Chamizal N MEM
33. Fort Davis NHS
34. Guadalupe Mountains NP
35. Lake Meredith NRA
36. Lyndon B. Johnson NHP
37. Padre Island NS
38. Palo Alto Battlefield NHP
39. Rio Grande WSR
40. San Antonio Missions NHP
41. Waco Mammoth NM

Big Bend NP

Check the list above if you have...
- *Visited Park*
- *Completed Junior Ranger Program*

There are stories of building homes that last a long time. There are stories about building bonds between people. And there are stories that explain how nature builds mountains, canyons, and sandy beaches.

Valles Caldera N PRES

It took thousands of hours to build the 72-foot high mound at Poverty Point NM and the city around it 3,000 years ago. Chaco Culture NHP shows that

Aztec Ruins NM

Pueblo people also built on a grand scale. **AT AZTEC RUINS, ONE HOUSE HAS 400 ROOMS.** Bandelier and El Morro national monuments preserve messages in rock carvings (petroglyphs). Petroglyph NM has one of the largest rock carving sites in North America. What do they mean? Some are sacred while others simply tell a story, but they should always be respected.

Capulin Volcano NM, Valles Caldera N PRES, and El Malpais NM, are places that show how the land was formed by volcanoes. The Big Room in Carlsbad Caverns NP is 4,000 feet long and 625 feet high. At White Sands NM, there are miles of glistening

Woolly Mammoth

warm waters at Hot Springs NP relax you after a busy day. At Waco Mammoth NM, you can help look for old bones. *A HERD OF MAMMOTHS ONCE LIVED WHERE THE PARK IS LOCATED TODAY.*

Cane River Creole NHP tells us about the life of slaves on a plantation and of their unique culture. San Antonio Missions NHP and Arkansas Post N MEM show us what happened when settlers moved to American Indian

Swamp life

white sand dunes. Jean Lafitte NHP has river swamps, twisting bayous, and lots of wildlife. Guadalupe Mountains NP includes the highest point in Texas.

That's a great thing about national parks: You can enjoy them while they protect the treasures of nature and history. Pecos NHP has hiking trails through the desert with prickly pear and yucca plants. Buffalo NR is one of nature's scenic rivers and remains untamed. No dams, just 135 miles of free-flowing rapids and pools. You can fish or swim in lakes behind dams at Chickasaw NRA and Amistad NRA. The soothing,

Many stories teach us valuable lessons. In the 1830s, President Andrew Jackson led an effort to move the Cherokee, Choctaw, and Chickasaw from their homelands. No one is sure how many died on the forced marches. Learn more about this tragic event at Fort Smith NHS. The effort to open Little Rock Central High School to all in 1957 was an important milestone in the civil rights movement. Nine brave African American students stood up for justice and the fight for equality.

San Antonio Missions NHP

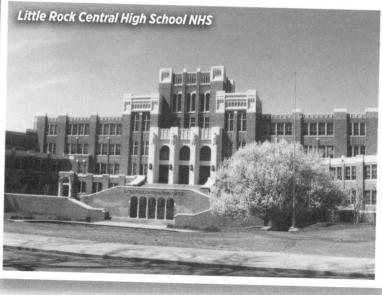

Little Rock Central High School NHS

land in the 1700s and 1800s. Sometimes, the struggle for land led to fights. Fort Davis and Fort Smith were built to protect settlers. Washita Battlefield NHS is the site where the U.S. Cavalry attacked a Cheyenne village.

SOUTHWEST REGION STICKERS AND PHOTOS

Place your Southwest Region Stickers (or any other stickers) on this page. You may also use this page to collect photos of your park trips or of the park rangers you meet!

PUT YOUR SOUTHWEST REGION OFFICIAL PARK CANCELLATIONS HERE!

MEM
2018
Southwest Region

PUT YOUR SOUTHWEST REGION OFFICIAL JUNIOR RANGER CANCELLATIONS HERE!

ROCKY MOUNTAIN REGION

What do people say about the Rocky Mountain parks?

Rocky Mountain NP

MONTANA

NORTH DAKOTA

SOUTH DAKOTA

WYOMING

UTAH

COLORADO

Bent's Old Fort NHS

COLORADO

- ① Bent's Old Fort NHS
- ② Black Canyon of the Gunnison NP
- ③ Colorado NM
- ④ Curecanti NRA
- ⑤ Dinosaur NM
- ⑥ Florissant Fossil Beds NM
- ⑦ Great Sand Dunes NP & PRES
- ⑧ Hovenweep NM
- ⑨ Mesa Verde NP
- ⑩ Rocky Mountain NP
- ⑪ Sand Creek Massacre NHS
- ⑫ Yucca House NM

MONTANA

- ⑬ Big Hole NB
- ⑭ Bighorn Canyon NRA
- ⑮ Glacier NP
- ⑯ Grant-Kohrs Ranch NHS
- ⑰ Little Bighorn Battlefield NM

NORTH DAKOTA

- ⑱ Fort Union Trading Post NHS
- ⑲ Knife River Indian Villages NHS
- ⑳ Theodore Roosevelt NP

SOUTH DAKOTA

- ㉑ Badlands NP

- ㉒ Jewel Cave NM
- ㉓ Minuteman Missile NHS
- ㉔ Mount Rushmore N MEM
- ㉕ Wind Cave NP

UTAH

- ㉖ Arches NP
- ㉗ Bryce Canyon NP
- ㉘ Canyonlands NP
- ㉙ Capitol Reef NP
- ㉚ Cedar Breaks NM
- ㉛ Glen Canyon NRA
- ㉜ Golden Spike NHS
- ㉝ Natural Bridges NM
- ㉞ Rainbow Bridge NM
- ㉟ Timpanogos Cave NM
- ㊱ Zion NP

WYOMING

- ㊲ Devils Tower NM
- ㊳ Fort Laramie NHS
- ㊴ Fossil Butte NM
- ㊵ Grand Teton NP
- ㊶ John D. Rockefeller, Jr., Memorial Parkway
- ㊷ Yellowstone NP

Arches NP

Check the list above if you have...
- ⬤ Visited Park
- ☐ Completed Junior Ranger Program

79

Bryce Canyon NP

They are big, wild, and sometimes miles from nowhere. They can be rough and rugged. You can see things there that are old, or not like anything else. Wonderful. Mysterious. Yet to some they are sacred and also their home. Let's take a closer look.

First, there are parks that are huge. Big land has space for big animals: grizzlies, elk, and bison. This is "big sky" country. There are tall mountains at Rocky Mountain NP and Grand Teton NP, deep canyons at Bighorn Canyon NRA, and untamed rivers at Missouri NRR. Glacier NP sits like a snowy crown at the top of a web of valleys and rivers that flow like ribbons in every direction. Jewel Cave NM is the world's third longest cave. At Bryce Canyon NP you can see incredible rock formations. Great Sand Dunes NP has the tallest dunes in North America. Rainbow Bridge NM contains one of the world's largest natural bridges.

Colorado NM is home for bighorn sheep, while prairie dogs and black-footed ferrets scamper about Badlands NP. Places like Zion NP are far from big cities and good for looking at stars aglow in inky black skies.

Grand Teton NP

Yellowstone NP

NP has a rock tower that looks like a pipe organ, more than 2,000 stone arches, and rocks that look like they could topple from any slight breeze. Yellowstone NP has pools of bubbling mud and colored pools of water. *THE FAMOUS GEYSER "OLD FAITHFUL" SHOOTS BOILING WATER MORE THAN 100 FEET INTO THE AIR.* Wind Cave NP has formations that look like spider webs while above ground there are bison, elk, and pronghorn antelope that can run faster than any other animal on the prairie. Of all the parks you will visit, none is like Mount Rushmore N MEM. It has the images of four U.S. presidents carved in a giant stone cliff.

What you see in many of these parks is old. It's hard to imagine just how old. Dinosaur NM, Fossil Butte NM, and Florissant Fossil Beds NM all contain signs of life from animals and plants that lived millions of years ago.

There are sites that make you stop and stare like the red rock domes of Capitol Reef NP. Colorful Arches

Wind Cave NP

It's good to remember that many parks were or still are the homelands of Plains, Plateau, and Pueblo tribes. Native peoples consider some park lands sacred. To find out more, visit Knife River Indian Villages NHS, Hovenweep NM, Devils Tower NM, and Mesa Verde NP. The explorers and pioneers who moved onto Indian lands in the 1800s brought their own ideas about land and how to live. This sometimes created trouble. Big Hole NB, Little Bighorn Battlefield NM, Fort Laramie NHS, and Sand Creek Massacre NHS preserve sites where fierce battles took the lives of families, soldiers, and warriors.

Golden Spike NHS

Bison

AT GOLDEN SPIKE NHS, YOU CAN LEARN ABOUT THE RAILROAD THAT LINKED EAST AND WEST IN 1869. Who built it? How did it change the lives of American Indians, the men who laid the tracks, and the travelers who rode the rails? Long lines of wagons still stirred up clouds of dust as they brought more and more settlers. The Indian tribes all along the railroad still tried to hold onto their ways of life. But that golden spike secured a future that no one could stop.

ROCKY MOUNTAIN REGION STICKERS AND PHOTOS

Place your Rocky Mountain Region Stickers (or any other stickers) on this page. You may also use this page to collect photos of your park trips or of the park rangers you meet!

PUT YOUR ROCKY MOUNTAIN REGION OFFICIAL PARK CANCELLATIONS HERE!

Bryce Canyon National Park

JUN 01 2018

Bryce, UT

PUT YOUR ROCKY MOUNTAIN REGION
OFFICIAL JUNIOR RANGER CANCELLATIONS HERE!

WESTERN REGION

The parks in Hawaii, California, Nevada, and Arizona protect amazing natural and historic places.

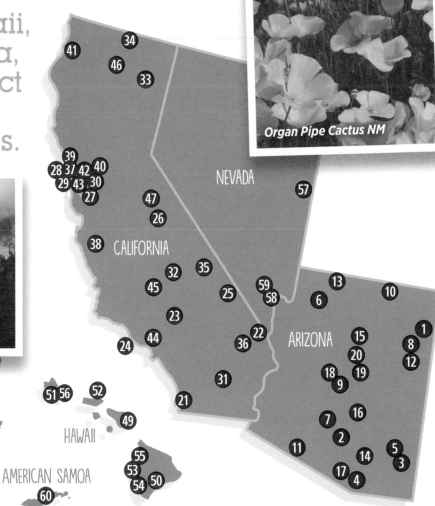

Organ Pipe Cactus NM

Yosemite NP

NEVADA

CALIFORNIA

ARIZONA

GUAM

HAWAII

AMERICAN SAMOA

ARIZONA

1 Canyon de Chelly NM
2 Casa Grande Ruins NM
3 Chiricahua NM
4 Coronado N MEM
5 Fort Bowie NHS
6 Grand Canyon NP
7 Hohokam Pima NM*
8 Hubbell Trading Post NHS
9 Montezuma Castle NM
10 Navajo NM
11 Organ Pipe Cactus NM
12 Petrified Forest NP
13 Pipe Spring NM
14 Saguaro NP
15 Sunset Crater Volcano NM
16 Tonto NM
17 Tumácacori NHP
18 Tuzigoot NM
19 Walnut Canyon NM
20 Wupatki NM

CALIFORNIA

21 Cabrillo NM
22 Castle Mountains NM
23 César E. Chávez NM
24 Channel Islands NP
25 Death Valley NP
26 Devils Postpile NM
27 Eugene O'Neill NHS

*Park is not open to the public.

28 Fort Point NHS
29 Golden Gate NRA
30 John Muir NHS
31 Joshua Tree NP
32 Kings Canyon NP
33 Lassen Volcanic NP
34 Lava Beds NM
35 Manzanar NHS
36 Mojave N PRES
37 Muir Woods NM
38 Pinnacles NP
39 Point Reyes NS
40 Port Chicago Naval
Magazine N MEM
41 Redwood NP
42 Rosie the Riveter/WWII
Home Front NHP
43 San Francisco Maritime NHP
44 Santa Monica Mountains NRA
45 Sequoia NP
46 Whiskeytown NRA
47 Yosemite NP

GUAM

48 War in the Pacific NHP

HAWAII

49 Haleakalā NP
50 Hawai'i Volcanoes NP
51 Honouliuli NM

Grand Canyon NP

52 Kalaupapa NHP
53 Kaloko-Honokōhau NHP
54 Pu'uhonua o Hōnaunau NHP
55 Pu'ukoholā Heiau NHS
56 World War II Valor
in the Pacific NM

NEVADA

57 Great Basin NP
58 Lake Mead NRA
59 Tule Springs Fossil Beds NM

AMERICAN SAMOA

60 National Park of American Samoa

Check the list above if you have...
○ *Visited Park*
□ *Completed Junior Ranger Program*

Sunset Crater Volcano NM

At Hawai'i Volcanoes NP, red-hot lava still oozes from the earth. At night it glows orange in the dark. Smoke and steam rise into the sky. When active, volcanoes throw bright globs of lava into the air. You also can see mountains, craters, and all sorts of strange shapes created by volcanoes and earthquakes on the mainland at Sunset Crater Volcano NM, Pinnacles NP, or Lava Beds NM.

While volcanoes form new land, water and wind wear away rocks and dirt. Grand Canyon NP may be the most famous place where you can walk over a mile deep into the earth. But there are other parks with canyons and rock towers like Canyon de Chelly NM.

Hawai'i Volcanoes NP

Lake Mead NRA has steep colorful cliffs while Petrified Forest NP has fossilized trees. Devils Postpile NM looks like it was built from gray, rock posts. Don't miss the "wonderland of rocks" at Chiricahua NM.

Over thousands of years, people called the deserts in this region home. They built the "great house" at Casa Grande Ruins NM. You can visit 700-year-old villages built into cliffs at Navajo NM, Tonto NM, and Walnut Canyon NM. At Tuzigoot NM, one pueblo (village) sits atop a hill, while at Wupatki NM, one is in the middle of the rust-red rocks of the Painted Desert. Don't forget, these parks still are an important part of people's lives.

Some 500 years ago explorers claimed this land for Spain. Contact with

Rosie the Riveter

World War II? *VISIT ROSIE THE RIVETER NHP TO LEARN MORE ABOUT THEM.*

Did these different people get along? How did they treat one another? The frontier outpost at Fort Bowie saw many battles between U.S. soldiers and the native Apache people. Hubbell Trading Post NHS is still run by the Navajo Nation and is within the Navajo Reservation. Pipe Spring NM preserves the homeland of the Paiute culture, later occupied by Mormons. See the island rock that became a prison at Alcatraz Island. Visit the ranch of labor leader César E. Chávez. You can hear stories of World War II bravery at WWII Valor in the Pacific NM and the fear and sadness that war creates at Manzanar NHS.

these outsiders changed life all over the region. Starting in the 1690s, Spanish priests built a string of missions (churches) including Tumacácori. In the 1770s, Juan Bautista de Anza led Spanish settlers all the way to San Francisco. At San Francisco Maritime NHP, you can visit ships built in the 1800s that sailed around South America to reach the West. Have you ever heard about the women who built ships during

What about the plants and animals that live in these states? How can they live in the desert? To find out, go to Organ Pipe Cactus NM, Death Valley NP, Joshua Tree NP, and Saguaro NP.

Cactus plants in the desert

Bighorn sheep

The shapes of the plants will surprise you. Careful, some will also stick you. To see how life is different along the coast visit Muir Woods NM, Golden Gate NRA, or Santa Monica Mountains NRA. Both Channel Islands NP and Haleakalā NP are in the Pacific Ocean, but they are not at all alike. Don't topple over when you look up at the giant redwood trees in Yosemite NP, Sequoia & Kings Canyon NP, or Redwood NP. At Tule Springs Fossil Beds NM you can learn about animals that are still alive today, as well as many that are extinct. Pinnacles NP is a good place to see falcons, eagles, and condors. The mountains, valleys, and meadows of Yosemite NP are home to wolves, grizzlies, mountain lions, and bighorn sheep.

Before you end your trip, enjoy one of the best things about national parks—the quiet. Castle Mountains NM and Mojave N PRES, are good places to slow down and relax. The sky above Joshua Tree NP fills with stars. The night is dark, but the heavens light to help you see.

Joshua Tree NP

WESTERN REGION STICKERS AND PHOTOS

Place your Western Region Stickers (or any other stickers) on this page. You may also use this page to collect photos of your park trips or of the park rangers you meet!

Put Your Western Region Official Park Cancellations Here!

PUT YOUR WESTERN REGION
OFFICIAL JUNIOR RANGER CANCELLATIONS HERE!

PACIFIC NORTHWEST AND ALASKA REGION

You can find adventure in Alaska and the Pacific Northwest—Washington, Oregon, and Idaho.

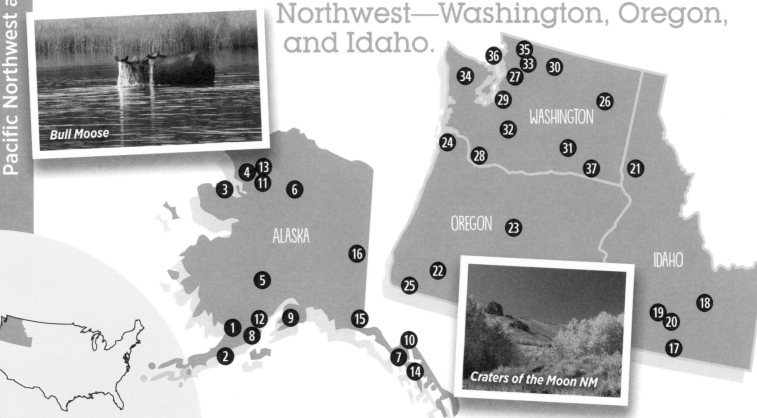

Bull Moose

Craters of the Moon NM

ALASKA

WASHINGTON

OREGON

IDAHO

Pacific Northwest and Alaska Region

Alaska

1. Alagnak WR
2. Aniakchak NM & PRES
3. Bering Land Bridge N PRES
4. Cape Krusenstern NM
5. Denali NP & PRES
6. Gates of the Arctic NP & PRES
7. Glacier Bay NP & PRES
8. Katmai NP & PRES
9. Kenai Fjords NP
10. Klondike Gold Rush NHP
11. Kobuk Valley NP
12. Lake Clark NP & PRES
13. Noatak N PRES
14. Sitka NHP
15. Wrangell-St. Elias NP & PRES
16. Yukon-Charley Rivers N PRES

Idaho

17. City of Rocks N RES
18. Craters of the Moon NM & PRES
19. Hagerman Fossil Beds NM
20. Minidoka NHS
21. Nez Perce NHP

Oregon

22. Crater Lake NP
23. John Day Fossil Beds NM
24. Lewis and Clark NHP
25. Oregon Caves NM & PRES

Washington

26. Lake Roosevelt NRA
27. Ebey's Landing NH RES
28. Fort Vancouver NHS
29. Klondike Gold Rush NHP
30. Lake Chelan NRA
31. Manhattan Project NHP
32. Mount Rainier NP
33. North Cascades NP
34. Olympic NP
35. Ross Lake NRA
36. San Juan Island NHP
37. Whitman Mission NHS

Denali NP & PRES

Check the list above if you have...
Visited Park
Completed Junior Ranger Program

The explorers Meriwether Lewis and William Clark reached the goal of their quest, the Pacific Ocean, in 1805. For shelter, they built Fort Clatsop, now in Lewis and Clark NHP. On the way, they learned about many tribes of American Indians including the Nez Perce.

In the early 1800s, traders used forts like Fort Vancouver to sell furs and buy supplies. Wagon trains of families moved west along the trails of explorers and American Indians. The tall, jagged peaks of

Lewis and Clark with Sacagawea

North Cascades NP

mountains within North Cascades NP show that travel was hard. It took muscle, sweat, and grit to move west.

Many dreamers didn't let the danger and hardship keep them from looking to the West. In the 1850s, farm families found new fields to plow at Ebey's Landing.

KLONDIKE GOLD RUSH NHP TELLS THE STORY OF STRIKE IT RICH FANTASIES. In the 1890s, men wanting to buy supplies swamped Seattle. Then they rushed off to places like Skagway, Alaska, to find gold.

This also is a land of natural wonders. When you visit Gates of the Arctic NP, you will see the darkest skies on earth. A dome of stars sparkles above. Lake Chelan NRA, Olympic NP, and Glacier NP have mountains with snow that lasts year-round. The tops of Mount Rainier NP and Denali NP often hide above the clouds. The deep bays at Kenai Fjords NP and Glacier Bay NP make fingers reaching into the land. Lake Clark NP looks like a huge, blue stone set in a ring of dark green forests. Wrangell-St. Elias NP is bigger than many countries.

John Day Fossil Beds NM

Prospector panning for gold

There also are surprises hiding under the colorful hills of John Day Fossil Beds NM, and Hagerman Fossil Beds NM. Animals that no longer exist once lived in Oregon and Washington State. Imagine it's 7,000 years ago. Can you picture the volcanoes that formed Crater Lake and Katmai national parks? Craters of the Moon NM shows the effect that exploding lava had on the land.

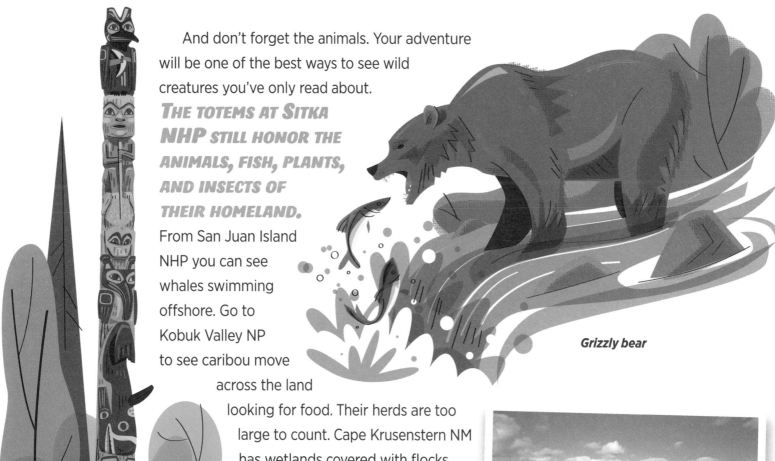

And don't forget the animals. Your adventure will be one of the best ways to see wild creatures you've only read about. **THE TOTEMS AT SITKA NHP STILL HONOR THE ANIMALS, FISH, PLANTS, AND INSECTS OF THEIR HOMELAND.** From San Juan Island NHP you can see whales swimming offshore. Go to Kobuk Valley NP to see caribou move across the land looking for food. Their herds are too large to count. Cape Krusenstern NM has wetlands covered with flocks of shorebirds. There are grizzly bears in Glacier NP catching fish along streams, and polar bears hunting seals in Bering Land Bridge N PRES.

Grizzly bear

Totem pole

Crater Lake NP

PACIFIC NORTHWEST AND ALASKA REGION STICKERS AND PHOTOS

Place your Pacific Northwest and Alaska Region Stickers (or any other stickers) on this page. You may also use this page to collect photos of your park trips or of the park rangers you meet!

PUT YOUR PACIFIC NORTHWEST AND ALASKA REGION OFFICIAL PARK CANCELLATIONS HERE!

PUT YOUR PACIFIC NORTHWEST AND ALASKA REGION OFFICIAL JUNIOR RANGER CANCELLATIONS HERE!

PARK ABBREVIATIONS

IHS	International Historic Site
NB	National Battlefield
NBP	National Battlefield Park
NBS	National Battlefield Site
NHP	National Historical Park
NHP & EP	National Historical Park & Ecological Preserve
NHP & PRES	National Historical Park & Preserve
NH RES	National Historical Reserve
NHS	National Historic Site
NL	National Lakeshore
NM	National Monument
NM & PRES	National Monument & Preserve
NMP	National Military Park
N MEM	National Memorial
NP	National Park

NP & PRES	National Park & Preserve
N PRES	National Preserve
NR	National River
NRA	National Recreation Area
NRR	National Recreational River
NRRA	National River & Recreation Area
N RES	National Reserve
NS	National Seashore
NSR	National Scenic River or Riverway
NST	National Scenic Trail
PWKY	Parkway
SRR	Scenic & Recreational River
WR	Wild River
WSR	Wild & Scenic River

JUNIOR RANGER PASSPORT
STICKER PAGE

Peel off these stickers and place them on the regional stickers pages inside your book!

MIDWEST REGION
Dayton Aviation Heritage NHP

SOUTHWEST REGION
Petroglyph NM

NORTH ATLANTIC REGION
Statue of Liberty NM

ROCKY MOUNTAIN REGION
Theodore Roosevelt NP

Explore Learn Protect

JUNIOR RANGER
EXPLORE · LEARN · PROTECT

PACIFIC NORTHWEST AND ALASKA REGION
Mount Rainier NP

MID-ATLANTIC REGION
Clara Barton NHS

WESTERN REGION
Redwood NP

GO TAKE A HIKE!

SOUTHEAST REGION
Martin Luther King, Jr., NHP

NATIONAL PARK SERVICE

NATIONAL CAPITAL REGION
Lincoln Memorial

USNPS